IMAGES
of Wales

PORTH

GATEWAY TO THE RHONDDA

A watercolour by Ian Penrick painted in 1855. This is the view Mr Evan Morgan had from Tynycymmer House around 1830. Note the Old Porth Bridge bottom right hand corner. The view is looking North to the Rhondda's Fawr and Fach.

Lewis Merthyr coal miners, c. 1900. Here we are at this moment in time and space, turning the pages and looking back at days gone by.

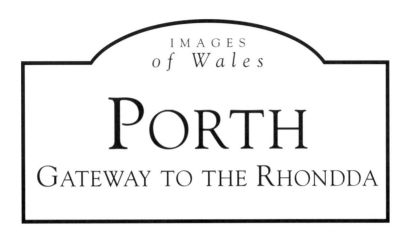

IMAGES
of Wales

PORTH
GATEWAY TO THE RHONDDA

Compiled by
Aldo Bacchetta and Glyn Rudd

TEMPUS

First published 2000
Copyright © Aldo Bacchetta and Glyn Rudd, 2000

Tempus Publishing Limited
The Mill, Brimscombe Port,
Stroud, Gloucestershire, GL5 2QG

ISBN 0 7524 2161 1

Typesetting and origination by
Tempus Publishing Limited
Printed in Great Britain by
Midway Clark Printing, Wiltshire

Dedicated to the mining Community of the Rhondda Valleys 1810-1990

Front cover illustration: *Thomas and Evans' soft drink bottling works.*
The building is now occupied by Avanti High Tech recording studio –
www.popfactory.com.

Contents

Topography   6

Foreword   7

Introduction   8

1. People and Places   9

2. Porth Fire Brigade and Mines Rescue Station   55

3. Thomas & Evans Welsh Hills Works   63

4. Sport and Leisure   81

5. Dinas to Gilfach Goch   99

6. Ynyshir and Wattstown   121

Acknowledgements   128

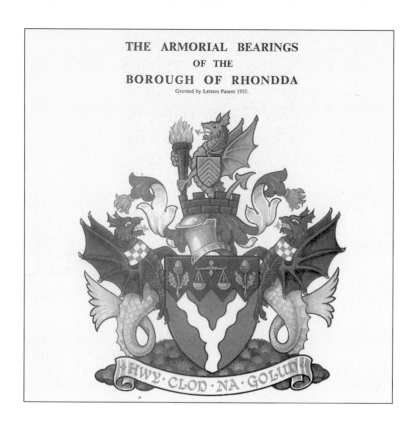

Topography

The Rhondda Urban District, with an area of 23,886 acres, is about 12 miles long by about 4 ¾ miles across at its widest part. It is irregularly oval in shape and consists of two valleys which gradually approach each other in their courses southwards and join at Porth, and thence the single valley so formed runs a short course before merging into the upper end of the Pontypridd Urban District at Trehafod.

The two valleys, together with the single valley continued after their junction, form an irregularly shaped 'Y'. The stem of the 'Y' extends from Porth to the boundary of the district at Trehafod, and is about one mile long, while the limbs are of unequal length. The longer, or Rhondda Fawr, valley is about 9 ½ miles long and the shorter, or Rhondda Fach, valley is about 6 ½ miles long.

The two limbs are separated by a steep ridge which rises from a point 600ft high just above Porth to an elevation of 1,692ft near the upper extremity of the district.

The valleys are traversed by rivers known as the Rhondda river in the stem of the above-described configuration and the Rhondda Fawr and Rhondda Fach rivers in the long and short valleys respectively. The bed of the Rhondda River at Trehafod is approximately 420ft above sea level, while the Rhondda Fawr River is at an elevation of 720ft at Blaenrhondda, and the Rhondda Fach River is at a height of 920ft at Maerdy.

The subsoil consists of Pennant sandstone overlying the coal-bearing strata, whilst in the few expanded portions of the valleys the soil is alluvial.

Foreword

Monday 28 January 1963 was our first visit to Porth, where I was to become, on Thursday 31 January 1963, the minister of the English Congregational Chapel (The Cong), and along with a young wife and three month old daughter (Bethan), were to be the new residents in 'The Manse'.

It was a cold winter's day, and we were God's frozen people. Our ravels had brought us from Swinton, Manchester, but a typical Rhondda welcome awaited us, with tea and welsh cakes. We remained at the church, now The United Reformed Church, for thirty three years, until retirement, and with our family being part of the church family, we were sad to leave. I have a nick name, 'Phillips of Porth, Bishop of Rhondda'. I have been blessed to preach to large congregations. Nan and the family have shared fully in the ministry.

Porth has been known as the producer of 'pop', what a taste, what a flavour! Our son Rhydian (Rib, in the boy band Mega), has worked with Avanti, the company who have bought the Thomas & Evans works, and are turning it once more into a 'Pop Factory', of a different kind.

It seems that I have touched so many lives in Rhondda, spheres of lives, coal, religion, politics, music, education, medicine and sport. Max Boyce says of 'The English Cong.' – 'I was there'. We feel that our stay at Porth has been long but very worthwhile.

I sit in Bacchettas' café, and recall the days that have gone by and the people who have made the Rhondda great, but now we must look forward to the Rhondda of the future. For Father's Day, I was given an old Corona bottle, complete with glass stopper. May the spirit of Porth long remain!

I have served in Porth and the Rhondda in many ways, preacher, magistrate, founder of the Citizens' Advice Bureau, organizer for The Blood Transfusion Service, collector and organizer for many causes, a chaplain to Hospitals, British Legion, United Services, SSAFA, and cancer research, one feels that they were all worthwhile.

From my family to your family, I pray God's blessing, and remember, 'Guide Me Oh Thou Great Jehovah'. My prayer to you from my column, Surgery for Souls, 'God be with you'.

Revd Keith Phillips JP
Broadcaster, lecturer, newspaper columnist,
President of the Rhondda Rotary Club, 1986/87.
4 July 2000

Introduction

As a schoolboy in far away North Carolina, we studied, as part of our Social Studies curriculum, geography and world history. The United Kingdom was then united and a great kingdom and we studied what each country in the kingdom produced or was noted for. When I read of the great coal mines and coke ovens in Wales, and the flames of revival that swept through this land, I dreamed I might visit that far off place and know more about a country like that. Well, not only was I permitted to visit here but to live, work and worship here. What a joy to get to know the people of the great Rhondda Valleys.

Aldo Bacchetta and Glyn Rudd have provided photographs, comments and insights into the glorious days of coal and coke and revival. It is a privilege to learn of your great history, tradition and family life. We are blessed to have men like Aldo and Glyn to keep reminding us of where we came from, because, if you don't know where you came from, you won't know where you are going.

'May the LORD's blessings be yours as you read this book.'

Revd Dr Edwin G. Moore JR, TH-G, PH.D, DD,
(Pastor of Bethany Baptist church, Ynyshir) seen above with Mrs Nina Moore.

One
People and Places

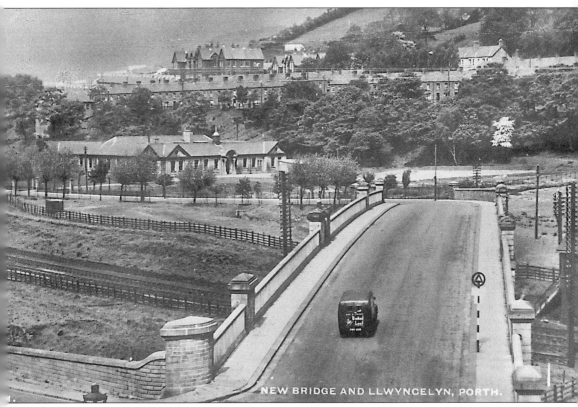

NEW BRIDGE AND LLWYNCELYN, PORTH.

The National Coal Board offices in the 1930s. Llwyncelyn School can be seen in the background.

A general view of Lewis Merthyr Collieries. On the left can be seen The Bertie, Trevor and Coedcae shafts. On the right the Hafod No. 1 and the Fairoak Hamlet.

First class steam coal being brought to the surface of Lewis Merthyr Colliery, 1924.

Left: Old and new headgears, Hafod No. 2 Pit, Trehafod. New headgear being erected over the shaft during the August bank holiday of 1924. *Right:* A colliery cage maintenance men inspecting the shaft at Lewis Merthyr Colliery, 1924.

Foraging for coal during the 1910 miner's strike. Included are: Ben Nicholas and his son John.

Rhondda Miners on strike in 1924. Second from the right is Frederick John Sparrow with his mates.

Great Western Colliery, Hopkinstown, 1910. Left to right are: Hetty shaft, No. 3 shaft and No. 2. Shaft. John Calvert, a Yorkshire man, sank this colliery in 1844. It took three years to reach the coal at a depth of 149yds. The Hetty shaft and engine house stands today as an industrial monument.

The Rhondda Urban Gas Works employees on Eirw Road, Britannia Road, Porth, 1909.

The Rhondda Gas Supply

The gasworks, prior to the year 1898, were owned by The Ystrad Gas and Water Company Limited, who commenced business in 1868. Under the provisions of a special Act of Parliament passed in 1896 the Urban District Council actually commenced operations on the 1 April 1898. Since then great strides have been made in an effort to improve the lighting, heating and cooking facilities of the area. The council has two gas works, one at Ystrad and the other at Porth, with distributing holders at Tonypandy and Treorchy. The quantity of coal carbonized annually is in the region of 16,000 tons, and the gas manufactured amounts to 185 million cubic feet. The works are capable of manufacturing gas of quality which satisfies the requirements of the Board of Trade and for the year ended 31 March 1939, the quality of gas supplied averaged 500 BThU, and is well suited to the requirements of the domestic and industrial consumers. The Undertaking has nearly 100 miles of mains, which serve 14,787 consumers.

In the early days, gas was only used for lighting, but modern developments have caused a steadily increasing use of gas for cooking and other domestic uses as well as for industrial heating purposes.

It would not be out of place to mention that the welfare of the Rhondda is mainly, if not solely, dependent upon mining and an increasing use of gas creates an increasing demand for coal, which in its turn naturally increases the possibilities for employment. Reliability of service is most important in lighting, and who will deny that gas has proved its reliability? 'Gas Never Fails' is very true in most aspects of daily utility and convenience.

Gas still plays an important part in artificial lighting and an up-to-date system of gas lighting is the best and the most suitable for large halls and public buildings, because apart from the fact of it being the most soothing and least harmful of any artificial lights to the eyes, the ventilation of the room is attained and down draughts are avoided.

An interesting fact, not so well known perhaps, is that our two most important national buildings, the Houses of Parliament and Buckingham Palace, are both provided with gas public lighting.

Cassie Thomas of 199 North Road, Porth, presenting an arm band to a telegram boy at Porth post office in the 1930s.

Employees at Porth post office in the 1930s.

Post office staff at Porth sorting office in 1933. This office closed in 1999 in the cause of efficiency, much to the dismay of the local community.

Post office staff in 1946. Included in the photograph are Fred Hallett, Trevor Thomas, Fred Haines, Mr Bassett, Bill Cowell and George Smith.

Porth. Station Street.

Station Street, Porth ... and the same view below, twenty-five years on. Note Lloyds Bank was then level with the road. Due to flooding the floor level has since been risen.

STATION STREET, PORTH.

Porth Taff Vale railway station, looking north in the 1900s.

Porth Great Western railway station, looking south in 1920.

Rhondda Fach Junction signal box, 1910. This was a busy and important control for the transportation of coal from the Rhondda to the South Wales Ports.

Porth House in all its grandeur with Mrs Hannah Griffiths and her maidservants in the 1900s. Hannah Street was named after her. This is now the site of the Alex Jones Day Centre, Station Street, Porth.

And ordnance survey map of Porth from 1863. Rheola Pub and old railway station can be locate top left. Porth Farm and Porth House with orchard now the site of the presence railway station are seen in the centre and bottom centre is Old Cymmer Chapel and National School for Boys and Girls. This was before the development of Porth as a commercial centre. Note there is no Hannah Street and no North Road.

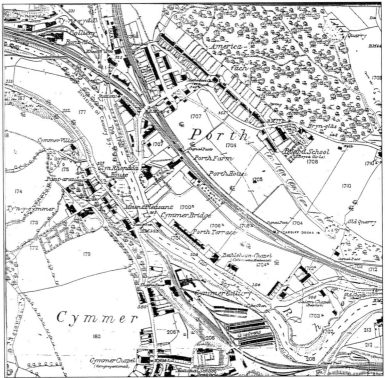

The completion of North Road Bridge in 1932. William Lawrence O'Flaherty of Trealaw is seen in the back row, far right.

Quarrying for stone at Cymmer Quarry in the 1890s. The stone was used for building chapels, houses, collieries and commercial properties.

FROM CYMMER TO CORNWALL

My great-grandparents, Evan Pearce and Jane Jones, née Williams, originally came from Abermawr, near Dolgellau. After being laid off in the North Welsh Slate Quarries, my great-grandfather became a coachman in Abermawr and eventually that job as well came to an end. So faced with unemployment, Evan wanted to emigrate with the family to Patagonia or the USA but Jane was a home bird who wanted to stay in Wales. So, a compromise was reached and south they moved. Firstly to Treorchy and then they finally settled in 36 Lincoln Street, Cymmer.

Evan started work as a miner in Insoles Cymmer Collier at around the middle of the First World War. My grandfather, also called Evan Pearce Jones, was around seven or eight years old when they moved to the Rhondda and really did not speak much English, only Welsh. In fact my great-grandparents were both first generation bilingual. The Jones's were a large family, six boys and two girls.

The eldest, Robert, was sent packing back to Abermawr for apparently being too religious. And wrong really, as it was Evan Jones Snr that later became a Baptist minister, although it was a few years of drinking and sinning before he finally saw the light.

Then there was Johnny, who was killed in 1915, in the battle of Loos, France, in the First World War, aged around nineteen. His mother, Jane, had a strange experience when one night there was a knock at the door at 36 Lincoln Street. She went to answer it and Johnny stood there and then disappeared. The following day she got a telegram to say that her second son had been killed in action. Ironically Loos was a French coal mining town.

Dai was the next son along with Evan Pearce next, my grandfather, then Watcyn Wyn who was called Silver because he had red hair. Welsh logic aye! and Owain Glyndwr and finally sisters Gweneth, who worked as a pastry cook at Thomas and Evans and Betty who was the youngeSt My grandfather, like most boys then, started work in Insoles Cymmer Colliery aged fourteen, with his father, in 1920. In 1922 his father Evan Snr, who at this time in his life was, as I mentioned earlier, a Baptist preacher in the Welsh Caer Salem Chapel in Cymmer, was killed as a result of a mine accident. The mine collapsed on him, crushing the side of his head. They later brought him up from the colliery and two week's later he died. I remember my grandfather saying, he did not want the same fate as his father, or to contract silicosis of the lungs. So, in 1923, he went to Bristol and lied about his age, then seventeen, and joined the marines to get out of the colliery. In the Service, he spent many years out east in China and Japan and later he was based at Tregantle Fort on the Rame Peninsular of Cornwall where he met my Cornish grandmother. After a few more years at sea and two daughter's later, Margaret and Elizabeth, he settled in the village of Millbrook, Rame Peninsula, Cornwall.

After leaving the marines he started work as a navvie, working on the roads and finally in the 1960s he ended his working life due to having a leg amputated as a truck driver. Throughout his life spent in Cornwall he only went back to the Rhondda a few times. The life he had back there was hard and I think brought back some bad memories. Even though he was a Welshman to the end, and proud of it, he felt the Celtic link between Cornwall and Wales was very much one of the same thing and consequently felt very at home in Cornwall. He died aged eighty-one in 1988.

His mother Jane left Wales only once in her lifetime, to make the journey to Cornwall to see her son and granddaughters. At arriving at Plymouth which is half a mile across the water from Cornwall, through fear, she could not cross the river Tamar on the Cremyll Ferry and so went all the way back to Wales without ever seeing where her son settled. As for myself, I went back to Wales, for the first real time in 1999 at the age of thirty-two and visited family places in the north and the Rhondda. I went to find Cymmer Collier and found it underneath a building to consumerism and Caer Salem Chapel, which had turned into flats and last 36 Lincoln Street where my journey ended, or started, whichever way you want to look at it. But strangely enough I felt very much connected and familiarised with the Rhondda. I guess hearing names and places from a young age you feel you know it in some way. But I guess like most things in life everything changes. Even though as a Welsh-Cornishman I won't forget my Welsh heritage. I realise that life for my family at 36 Lincoln Street back then was a damn site harder than it is today and I for one would not have wanted to experience the hardship of life in the Rhondda Valley Collieries, or indeed, the Cornish mines.

Andrew Penhaligan
April 2000

Left: Mr Evan Jones (1907-1988), father of Andrew Penhaligan. Engraved on his headstone are the words, 'Peidiwch Am Hanghofio' which means, 'Do not forget me'. *Right:* Mr Andrew Penhaligan outside the house in which he was born at 36 Lincoln Street, Cymmer.

The children of 'William the Milk' from Victoria Terrace, 1935. Janet is seen with her brothers David, Trevor and Eban (seated on a stool). They were photographed at Barry Island and look very glum as they were impatient to go to the funfair.

Nylon socking repairers of Blossoms Ltd, Cymmer Yard, Porth, 1 September 1949. Left to right, back row: Valmai Thomas, Lilian Light, Sylvia James, Jean Jones, Pat Nickolas, Eileen Gover, Mavis Williams. Middle row: Iris Williams, Marjorie Blackmore, Maureen Walters, Rita Macey, Violet Hutchinson, Irene Old, Violet Stuckey, Audrey Bailys, Tina Martin, V.S. Humphries, Peggy Painter, Jean English, Bron Morris, Pat O'Hara, Clara Harvey, Mrs Jones, Irene Rowlands, Margaret Baragweruth. Front row: Rita Mortimer, Doreen Davies, Betty Harris, Mildred, Joan Dallimore, Maureen McCarthy, Mavis Chapman.

Cymmer Prize Jazz Band at the rear of High Street, Cymmer and Glynfach, 1926. The band were making the most of it during the long strike

Cymmer Junior Mixed School, 1936. The teacher on the left is Mr Rossiter.

Left to right, back row: C/Sgt J. Hancock, C/Sgt T.G. Evans, Sgt T. Parry, Sgt F. Carlson, Sgt P. Cowley, Sgt A.J. Portal, Sgt F. Poutney, Sgt K. Parker, C/Sgt P. Williams. Second row from the back: Sgt W.J. Boyce, Sgt T.M. Harris, Sgt J.L. Sullivan, Sgt D.T. Morgans, Sgt F.H. Hellyar, Sgt H.R. Dobbins, Sgt J.M. Rogerson, Sgt V.G. Rees. Third row: CSM J.A. Collyer, Sgt M.B. White, Sgt W.H. Baker, Sgt L. Flook, Sgt R.A. Lloyd, C/Sgt R.H. Lodwick, Sgt V. Fletcher, Sgt T.J. Green, Sgt D. Batchelor, Sgt D.R. Jones, CSM A.E. Wilmott. Front row: CSM J. Mansfield, CSM J.F. Woods, Brig. F.P. Barclay DSO MC (Bde Comd), RSM A.K. Pyke, Field Marshal The Viscount Montgomery KG KCB DSO, Col, Sir R.G. Llewellyn CB CBE MC TD DL JP (Honorary Colonel), Lt-Col. P.C. Hinde DSO (Commanding Officer), Bandmaster A.H. Trotman, CSM C. Storey, CSM T.H. Fitch.

Sixth Platoon, 'A' Company, South Wales Borderers, at Bogloaia, Italy, in 1942. Mog Davies of Cymmer is fifth from the left, second row.

24

Royal Welsh Fusiliers, 1st Batallion, leaving Jamaica, 1950. Included in this photo fourth from right, front row, is Alfred Martin. Second from the right, front row, is Bill Roach, better known as Ken Barlow of *Coronation Street*.

Aldo and Mario Bacchetta in Berlin in 1957. They are seen being interviewed by Reg Dixon of the BBC for British Forces Family Favourites.

VE day party at Fountain Terrace, Trehafod, 1945.

Children from Charles Street, Porth, 1931. Left to right, back row: Ceridwen Jones, Cath Griffith, Eira Evans, Marie Thomas, Betty Ashford. Second row from the back: Iris Leyshon, Dennis Hale, Renee Brown. Third row: Mair Thomas, Dorcy Galey, Myra Jenkins, Peggy Griffiths, Lilian Barnett, Joan and Connie Dent, Nancy Evans. Front row: Billie Williams, Len Alford, Dilwyn Jones, Gordon Thomas, Terry Hopkins.

Porth Woolworth girls with manager Mr Fisher in 1947.

Porth Woolworth outing to Swansea, 1947.

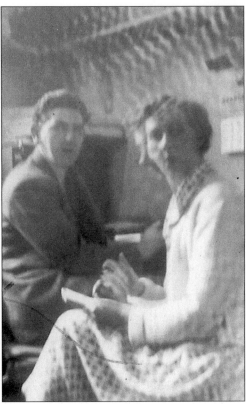

Left: Mr Abe Moore, Deputy Area Dust Suppresser Engineer taken at the NCB offices, Llwyncelyn, 1956. *Right:* Mr Vernon Williams and Secretary Clarice, NCB offices, Llwyncelyn, 1956.

Mr Vernon Williams and Anthea Tucker taken at the Lewis Merthyr Colliery Offices, 1956.

Pauline Ware and Anthea Tucker pictured by the Power House, Lewis Merthyr Colliery, 1961.

Bethania Band of Hope, 1920/21. The conductor was Mr T.J. Morgan.

Ministers and Deacons from the Rhondda Deacons Fellowship, 1947.

English Congregational chapel choir 1936. The conductor was John Davies, TTSC 1885-1949.

Lord Tonypandy, Allan Rogers MP and the Revd Keith Phillips JP pictured at the unveiling of memorial at Cymmer Colliery site 6 November 1988. This was in memory of the 114 miners killed on 15 July 1856.

St David's night celebrated at The English Congregational church, Porth, 1 March 1972.

Left: The actress Miss Rachel Thomas and Mrs Margaret Millington pictured at the Centenary Celebrations of The United Reformed church, Porth, formerly The English Congregational church 1885-1995. *Right:* Mrs Nan Phillips, wife of the Revd Keith Phillips, Miss Freda Travess and Miss Margaret Sendell taking part in the Centenary Celebrations.

Mair Healy, Pat Carpenter, Reg Healy, Alf Carpenter and the Rev. Keith Phillips at the Centenary Celebrations of The United Reformed Church.

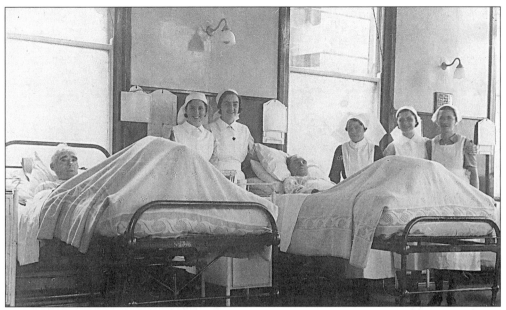

A Porth hospital ward in 1950. The hospital opened in 1894 and closed in 1999. It has now been earmarked as a private nursing home.

Left: Porth Hospital in 1950. Charge Nurse Hywel Johns and Staff Nurse Evans. *Right:* Porth Hospital Annexe. Pictured are Nurses Mair Jones and Ann Rosser.

Doctor and Mrs Clarke's House and Surgery, Porth, 1940.

Dr Clarke's Diary – 1926-1965

Patents on the dole paid 3d a week to the GP. Businessmen 'and the like' two guineas a year. 'We worked all the hours God sent. Doctors today don't know they're born', said eighty-eight-year-old Dr John Clarke, a Rhondda doctor from 1926 until 1965. A full night's sleep was rare and only with NHS patient registration in 1948 did he and his partner discover 12,000 souls on their books! That 3d (1p now) covered the person on the dole and his family for he doctor's services and operations in the 100 bed Porth Hospital. 'When I went to the Rhondda not a single maternity bed existed in the valley. All the babies were born at home, dead or alive', said Dr Clarke, a Scot, whose Porth Farm practice was one of the best known in the Rhondda.

'The NHS made little difference to me. I always dealt with working people and I was a colliery doctor. You were close to the people. You knew all the gossip, who was sleeping with whom. People did not have such high expectations then. They were more appreciative. You'd give a tonic – something with iron in it – and the nastier it tasted the better they liked it. In those days you had gamps – women of experience sent for in time of need. They would help when babies were born or lay out the dead or when people were sick. Some of them could not read or write, but they nursed quite well and often helped me.

'I remember fighting compensation cases for miners. Many of them died of silicosis. I performed post mortems. Did them on a kitchen table or in the coffin. I'd put the lungs in a biscuit tin and send them to Cardiff.'

Dr Clarke, who wife, Maud, earned £5 19s (£5.95) for three months' work at Swansea General and Eye Hospital in the early 1920s, owned a 12-horsepower Clyno car. 'Had to be able to get about', he said. 'I once delivered five babies before breakfast, two sets of twins and one other. We made more house calls in those days because many people were nursed at one whereas today they might be in hospital. Pneumonia was a big killer, and there was scarlet fever and diphtheria. In the days before the NHS, Dr Clarke earned up to £2,500 a year – around £32,000 today.

'Up to 1948 I performed 90 per cent of my own operations – hernias, tonsils and adenoids, appendectomies, caesarean births. I remember once there were six lots of tonsils to be removed and six circumcisions. There was a bit of a mix-up on the last two and instead of removing this wee lad's tonsils, I circumcised him. His mother said that there was something wrong down below and we realised the mistake. We made a new appointment for the tonsils and, anyway, the circumcision did him no harm. Couldn't get away with it today.

'People say funny things. I once asked a Porth woman how often she breast-fed her baby. 'Every time he cries" she said, 'and all the time in the pictures'. Odd things happen too. I once had an old dispenser, Pop Williams. He must have been seventy, and one day he disappeared leaving his pension book behind. The police dragged the river for him but there was no sign. Two years later they found him dead in the attic of my partner's house. There he was, propped up wearing a trilby, spectacles and reading a cowboy story'.

Dr Clarke a farmer's son from Keith in Scotland's Grampian country now lives in Talbot Green. He was one of a great influx of Scottish doctors into the valleys, he knew both A.J. Cronin, author of *The Citadel*, a doctor's story set in the coalfield of the1920s and .J. Cook, renowned miner's leader of the same era. His two grandsons are doctors while two granddaughters are pharmacists, but he himself is the last of his line. 'Every doctor practising in the Rhondda Valley when I started is dead, bar me. No. I never yearned to go back to my 'ean folk', said the doctor, adding with a chuckle, 'because I was doing quite nicely here'.

Nowadays, he said, doctors pay £1000 a year for medical insurance to protect them from lawsuits. 'I never paid more than two guineas'. The National Health Service, he reckons, should get more cash. 'The Chancellor should put more money into it instead of taking two pence off tax'.

Doctor and Mrs John Clarke enjoying their retirement at Talbot Green.

North Road, Porth, preparing for the Royal visit of Edward, Prince of Wales in 1936.

Left: Twins, Mario and Aldo Bacchetta with brother Renato pictured with their Nannie, Edna May Walters in Porth Park, 1937. *Right:* A Sunday School parade passing the Rhondda Hotel in 1940.

A large group of Rhondda Miners enjoying a rare break. Many of these would be attending Porth Surgery for medical attention under Dr John Clarke.

Maynard Davies Angling Club Presentation Dinner at Gambarini's Restaurant, Porth, 1957. Left to right, standing: Dick Owen, Ken Bence, Elfed Aubrey, Mr Davies (Lloyds Bank) Mr Maynard Davies (Area General Manager NCB) Dr Bill King, V. Harveson, H. Williams, Police Sergeant Bill Davies, Police Inspector Bill Jones, W. Aldgate.

Maynard Davies Angling Club Presentation Dinner at Gambarini's Restaurant, Porth, 1958. Left to right, back row, standing: E. Williams, Dr Ed Worthy, Doug Davies, V. Haverson, J. Perry, W. Jones, A. Bale, Horace Williams, G. John (Manager of Boots, Porth), G. Mitchell, Mr Edwards, B. Owen, Dr King, E. Aubrey, B. Newell, B. Lawson, K.A. Bence, W. Aldgate, Ralph Thomas, I. Jones. Front row, seated: Dr Williams, Colin Samuel, D. Davidson, W. Lewis.

Maynard Davies Angling Club Presentation Dinner at Gambarini's Restaurant, Porth, 1959. Left to right, back row, standing: Gwyn Mitchell, G. Aubrey, H. Williams, Ken Bence, Dick Owen, Elfed Aubrey, Mr Thomas, Mr Newell. Front row, seated: Dr Ed Worthy, Dr Edwards, V. Harveson, Dr King, Bob Davies.

Left: Mr Elfed Aubrey with his salmon, a record catch for the year 1962 on the River Usk at Llanover. *Right:* Mr Ron Bacchetta, Chairman of the Porth Chamber of Trade.

Eglwys Calfaria chapel, North Road, Porth, 1950. Seated front left is Mr Newell, chemist of Hannah Street, Porth.

Glamorgan County Council Election

THURSDAY, MARCH 7th, 1946.

Electoral Division of Porth.

The Workers' Champion

Labour's True Friend

Vote for DAN JONES

The People's Candidate

Printed and Published by D. John Jones, Electric Press, Porth.

Glamorgan County Council Election

THURSDAY, MARCH 7th, 1946.

TO THE ELECTORS OF THE PORTH DIVISION.

LADIES AND GENTLEMEN,

For the last nine years I have had the honour of serving you as your representative for this division and during this period it has been my honest endeavour to serve you to the best of my ability, and to do all in my power to safeguard your interests.

It is with the utmost confidence, therefore, that I again offer you my services, and solicit your further support and vote at the forthcoming County Council Election.

With the end of World War II, and the dawn of peace, many problems will arise—the usual aftermath of world conflicts—and one of the greatest of these will be that of finding work for each and every member of the various Services on demobilisation. We owe a deep debt of gratitude to these men and women, and are under a great obligation to them. I am fully conscious of this, and would assure them, if such an assurance is necessary, that I shall do all in my power to see that the heroes of 1939-1945 are reinstated in their former pre-war employment, or found suitable work, with the least possible delay after their release from the Forces.

My past record will show that I have always supported the various movements for the establishment of NEW INDUSTRIES in the Rhondda, thus reducing the ranks of the unemployed, and I am not unmindful of the great need of alternative employment for the men who have been maimed in the mines, and who have been compelled to leave the collieries, owing to disablement by diseases peculiar to the mining industry. These men must not be allowed to become derelict, but must be found congenial employment as near as possible to their homes.

Our Educational system is undergoing great changes, and whilst we must advance with the times, I am of the opinion that the local autonomy enjoyed by the Rhondda Education Committee, and wielded with much wisdom and success in the past, must not be prejudiced, and I shall do everything possible to assist the Local Education Authority to retain its full rights and freedom of action.

I have been the President of the local Old Age Pensioners Association since its inception, and have always fought for the betterment of their conditions. Needless to say, my sympathies and support may always be relied on by the aged.

Although the main responsibility for providing adequate Housing accommodation rests with the local Authority, it is the concern of the County Council as well, and this very acute problem will always command my earnest consideration and support.

During my period of office as your representative I continuously agitated for the abatement of the flooding nuisance at Trehafod, and I am happy to be able to state that the completion of the improvements in this area have practically eliminated all risks of further flooding.

Should you do me the honour of again returning me as your representative, I shall continue to watch your interests with the same care and devotion as I have always exercised in the past.

I remain, yours faithfully,

DAN JONES

173 ABER-RHONDDA ROAD,
PORTH.

RHONDDA URBAN DISTRICT COUNCIL ELECTIONS--Ward 11
THURSDAY, MAY 8th, 1952   Polling from 8 a.m. to 9 p.m.

You have TWO Votes

VOTE FOR
THE
Two Official Labour Candidates

Mr. EVAN EDWARDS   Mr. ALFRED T. ALLEN

Labour believes in Britain !

Keep faith with the Labour Party

Left: Labour candidates in 1952.
Below left: A certificate from the Mining and Engineering School,.
Below right: Cross Keys Hotel which was the meeting place for many political rallies and debates during the general strike of 1926.

Glamorgan County Council.

EDUCATION COMMITTEE.

Summer

Mining & Engineering School

held at

Cardiff

August, 1921

This is to Certify that

Alfred T. Allen

diligently attended and satisfied the Examiners in the Course in

Electrical Engineering of Collieries.

Mining Engineering, Mining Drawing and Engineering Science

Signed,

John James.

Chief Education Official.

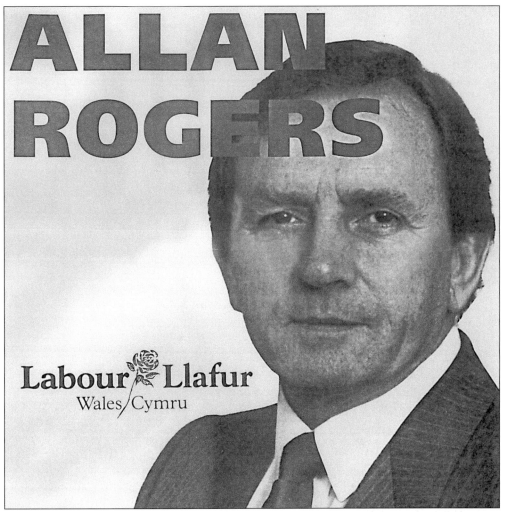

ALLAN ROGERS

Labour 🌹 Llafur
Wales/Cymru

Allan Rogers BSc, FGS, MP from the Rhondda. Allan Rogers and his wife, Ceridwen, have four children. The son of an ex-Rhondda miner, his father and seven brothers worked in the mines.

Allan has served Rhondda as its MP since 1983 and previously was the Member of the European Parliament for South East Wales from 1979 to 1984 serving as Vice-President of the European Parliament 1979 to 1981. He was appointed as and External Professor, at University of Glamorgan in 1996. He also served on the Public Accounts Committee and on the Select Committee for Welsh Affairs, Shadow Minister of State for Defence from 1987 to 1992 and Shadow Minister of State for Foreign and Commonwealth Affairs from 1992-1994.

He was appointed by the Prime Minister in 1994 to the Intelligence and Security Committee responsible to the Prime Minister for the oversight of the administration, finance and policy of the Secret Service Agencies – MI5, MI6 and GCHQ. He also worked as a geologist in Canada, USA and Australia and in the UK for the Coal Board. Between 1970 and 1979 he was District Secretary for the Workers Educational Association in South Wales.

Between 1965 and 1979 he had wide experience as a District and County Councillor. He was Chairman of the Governors of the Polytechnic of Wales, Vice-Chairman of the Mid Glamorgan Education Authority, a Member of the Mid Glamorgan Health Authority, the Welsh Joint Education Committee and the National Advisory Council for Adult and Continuing Education.

PORTH COUNTY
Go

Porth Secondary Grammar Mixed School, November 1957.

PORTH GRAM
GO

Porth Secondary Mixed School, July 1960.

MIXED SCHOOL.
ni

Panora Ltd.
Phone—CHANCERY 2779
56 Eagle Street,
London, W.C.1.

CAL SCHOOL
NI

Standard 2 at Islwyn School, Mount Pleasant, Porth in 1946. Second from the right is Joan Coburn, now Mrs Mike Poole, and in front is Jean Welsh, now Mrs Curtis.

Mount Pleasant, Porth, Old Age centre. Included in the photograph are: Mrs Florrie Sutton with grandson Mark, Mrs Ivins, Mrs Hughes, Mrs Harris, Queenie Owens, Tom Jones, Mr and Mrs Pugh, Mr and Mrs Salt, Mrs Head, Mrs Deer, Nancy Wilding.

Islwyn Infants' School, 1936. Left to right, back row: Tommy Rabbit, Kerry Smart, Danny Davies, David James. Second row from the back: John Sutton, Heulwyn Thomas, Joyce Vicary, Margaret James, Elisabeth Ishma, Sylvia James, Mary Parry, Valmae Parry, Douglas Sanays. Third row: Fred Knight, Gwenda Harcoombe, Mair Head, Sylvia Edmunds, Evelyn Harcoombe, Maureen Owens. Front row: Raymond Roberts, Peter Lewis, Erni Briar, Dougie Ring.

Rhondda Transport Dinner, Judges Hall, Tonypandy, 1940. Mr Harry Welch is seen in the second row, second from right. He was chairman of the Rhondda Transport and General Workers Union and formed this branch.

Rhondda Transport tram shed with maintenance crew, 1908.

Rhondda Transport Inspectors' bull-nosed Cowley car, 1929.

Tom Hanley and Mog Richards, two of Rhondda Transport's drivers, 1930.

Rhondda Transport drivers and conductors standing beside AEC coach, 1950. Vernon Fletcher is second from the left.

Employees Rhondda Transport Company. 'Off with Hymns and Arias' on route to Holyhead to see the big game at Dublin, 1953. The bus driver, W.L. Jones, seen in the front row on the right.

RTC v. South Wales Transport at St Helens, Swansea, for the BET Shield, 1936. The Lord Mayor of Swansea is in the centre, middle row. Jerry Lynch (first left, middle row) scored the winning try.

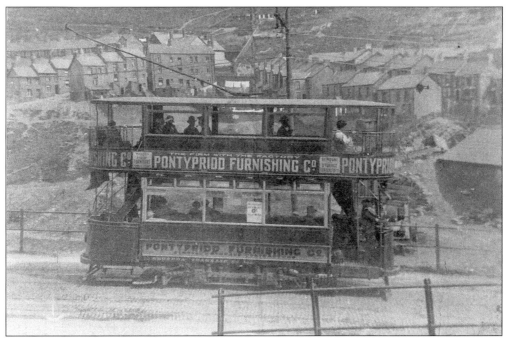

One of he first trams heading for the depot in Porth, 1908. The village in the background is Stanleytown. Note the linen on the line, the houses were used as lodgings for the workforce that occupied the valley at that time.

Left: Mr Frank Ferrari and granddaughter Francesca behind the counter at Ferrari's Café, Hannah Street, Porth, 1984. *Right:* Mrs Francis Ferrari and daughter Louisa standing by the original Italian frothy coffee espresso machine in the café, 1984.

Mrs Ferrari and assistant Margaret Rudd having a quiet little chat before Frank comes back in 1980!

Mrs Jones with her daughter Dolly. Many years ago they owned the transport café on the corner of the Rhondda Transport Depot, Tynewydd Square, Porth.

Porth Square during the floods of 1920. Note the tramlines and the tram stranded on the hill.

Rhondda Fach river burst its banks and flooded the rear of 'Norman's' The Garage, Aberrhondda Road. The Wolesley car belonging to Mr Densley, manager of Charles Jenkins Timber Yard, can be seen almost afloat, 1961.

Rhondda Trades Union Council (TUC) in the 1940s. Left to right, back row, standing: C. Elford (EC member), S.J. Havard (organizer), R.G. Cook (organizer), J.G. Tucker (organizer), H. Welch (EC member), Wm Howlett (organizer), W.J. Forbes (EC member), J. Holbrook (EC member). Front row, sitting: R.M. Evans (organizer), H. Orchard (trustee), J. Philips (trustee), G. Lloyd (District President), W.E. Hopkins (District Secretary), R.G. Lewis (organizer), R.G. Smith (EC member). Sitting at front is Miss C.E. Wallbridge (Minute Secretary).

Battle of Britain Celebration Committee, Aberrhondda Road, Porth. Left to right, back row: Mrs Isaacs, Mrs Denty, Nora Adams, Mrs Coburn, Dulcie Honey, Ceridwen Williams, Gwennie Blewitt. Front row: Lilian Sims, Mrs S.A. Welch, Chairperson, Greta Williams, Mrs Williams, Mrs Gould, Mrs Lynch, Joan Roberts.

Two

Porth Fire Brigade and Mines Rescue Station

The Merryweather motorized fire appliance came into service in 1912, replacing the previous horse-drawn machine. The local Porth Fire Brigade was formed by the Porth Chamber of Trade in 1896. The first Captain was the late William Evans of Thomas and Evans Grocers and Corona Pop fame. Thomas and Evans' horses were fetched from their stables in Jenkin Street, Porth when there was a fire call for the horse drawn appliance. William Evans presented the first motorised fire appliance to Porth Fire Brigade in 1926. Europe's first steam appliance was built in London in 1829. Merryweather produced their first steam pump fire appliance in 1861. Despite this invention production of manual pumps continued into the late 1860s.

Parochial records from St John The Baptist Church, The Hayes, Cardiff show that, as far back as 1739, a manual fire appliance was kept in the porch of the church tower for use by the Parish for fire fighting and that a bell in the tower was rung on the occasion of a fire.

Ivor Morgan, Porth Fire Fighter, 1906.

Fire at Llwyncelyn School, Porth, 1907.

Fire fighters at Llwyncelyn School, 1907. Second from the left Ivor Morgan.

Porth Fire Brigade in 1909. Ivor Morgan is seen back row, third from left.

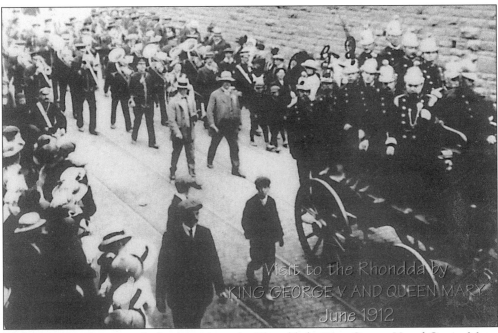

Porth Fire Brigade on parade for the visit to the Rhondda by King George V and Queen Mary, June 1912.

Mr Gwyn Harries with the Merryweather Fire Fighting Appliance at Porth Fire Station Open Days, 1999.

The crew of fire fighters dressed in the old uniforms for a local wedding in 1999. Left to right, back row: Station Officer Robert England, Leading Fireman Gerald Williams. Front row: Fire Fighter Ceri Jones, Leading Fire Fighter Michael Evans, Fire Fighter Colin Pritchard, Fire Fighter Adrian Rowlands.

Dinas rescue station as it was in 1912.

The Mines Rescue Station

Due to the frequency of mining disasters in Great Britain, a part of the Coal Mines Act of 1911 made provision for colliery owners to provide Central Rescue Stations. The Rhondda Collieries Rescue Association, which represented more than 20 Mining Companies owning some 73 collieries, opened its Rhondda rescue station on 27 June 1912, through a visit of King George V and Queen Mary.

The location of the Rhondda station at Dinas is only 200yds from the first shaft sunk in the valley by Walter Coffin. The building contractors were Messrs Niblett and Davies of Cardiff who built the station at a cost of £3,448 17s 3d. The station served some 73 collieries, 54 of them major undertakings in Rhondda, and was considered at the time one of the largest in Great Britain. In 1913 coal output from Rhondda – mainly for export – was 9,610,705 tonnes.

The inevitable, but premature, decline of the Rhondda and South Wales coalfield was never reflected in the operation of the Dinas rescue station because it continued to develop by the successive closure of other Rescue Stations in South Wales.

The station duty room is manned 24 hours a day and is able to turn out immediately at least one team of rescue men, fully equipped with a rescue officer.

Dinas first rescue crew and appliance, which was a converted fire engine, 1912.

Margaret Thatcher, before she was Prime Minister, visiting Dinas rescue station. Left to right. back row: Allan Green, Les Hughes, Ray Amber, Gordon Richards, Bob Griffiths, Billy King, Glen Thomas. Front row: Albert Kelk (third officer), Barry Hall (Asst Supt.), Malcolm 'Mal' Davies (Supt).

Mines rescue station, seen in the 1950s, with concrete houses above and Porth Textile Factory on the right.

Canaries kept at the rescue station. These birds are still used today because they continue to be one of the best methods of detecting gas in a mine.

Three
Thomas & Evans
Welsh Hills Works

William Thomas was born in Marthry, Pembrokeshire, in 1851. This was a hilltop village which had been occupied since prehistoric times. An old cromlech and some standing stoned are to be found within the parish boundaries. Roughly circular walls encircle the church which was dedicated to the holy martyrs names Marthry and Merthyr. They were buried in stone coffins. The church was rebuilt in 1867 and inside there is a charter from Edward III. There is a weekly market and a Michaelmas Fair is held to this day.

William came from a farming family and went in for butchering. At fourteen he went to Newport in Monmouthshire as an apprentice. In 1874 he married Rowena Rowland and moved to Aberbeeg. There he built a small butcher's shop with living accommodation above and called it 'Gold Tops' after the area in Newport where he had served his apprenticeship.

As the business developed he found he needed more space and so built a warehouse, a bigger shop and with a growing family, more living accommodation.

In 1882 a young William Evans, whose roots were in Pembrokeshire came to work in the shop and lived with the family for three years. Some years later the two men went into partnership to produce bottled soft drinks which were distributed from Porth all over South Wales under the name of 'Thomas & Evans'. The partnership was financed by William Thomas who lent £238 (at 50% interest!) Some years later when William Evans wished to expand William Thomas urged caution and the partnership was amicably dissolved. The firm sold out in the 1950s to Corona who were in turn bought up by Beechams for what, by our standards, must have been a lot of money.

Left: William Evans Esq, JP, CC, Founder and Governing Director of Thomas & Evans (1885-1934). *Right:* D. Frank Evans Esq, JP, Chairman and Managing Director of Thomas & Evans (1935-1940).

Left: J.L. Thomas Esq, chairman of Thomas & Evans (1940-1951). *Right:* W.O. James Esq, Managing Director from 1940.

This imposing Welsh Hills Mineral Waters Factory was built in the 1890s to cater for the wide demand after William Evans had broadened his activities to include the manufacture of soft drinks. Located on the edge of Porth, it stood for years as a symbol of success and modern production techniques but now belongs to a bygone age. The building is currently being restored to its former glory and is to be transformed into a high-tech state of the art recording studio by the Avanti Television Company, under the 'Fizz' label and can be reached on www.popfactory.com.

Thomas & Evans

Reliable transport was a *sine qua non* of Thomas & Evans' grocery and soft drinks trade – not only to depots and retail outlets but also in direct delivery to customers' doorsteps. Transport was vital not only in distribution but also to ensure that the productive processes of his many and various factories were properly fed by an unbroken flow of raw materials transported at lowest cost. William Evans was keenly aware of the significance of transport and proud of his facilities, which explains why, just after the turn if the century, he chose to highlight in his advertisements that two steam engines and two hundred horses were being used in his business. The steam engines, of mammoth proportions, were a sight not to be forgotten. They ponderously hissed, chugged and crunched their way on the narrow, steep and winding Rhondda roads hauling their wagons heavily laden with mineral waters behind, and preceded by the man with the red flag who was then required by law. Mr David Iles, at sixteen years of age, was one of two employed in this capacity to warn anyone in its path of the approach of the juggernaut. He regularly blazed the trail in fair and foul weather on a three-day round trip from Porth to Maesteg and back, and suffered himself, injury to a foot which somehow got beneath one of the gigantic solid wheels.

The horses too were impressive, particularly on May Day when, groomed to perfection, they were paraded in their hundreds around the streets of Porth. The steam engines, or 'steamers' as they were sometimes called, were discarded in the 1920s but the horse-drawn pop carts of distinctive design, bright red colour and gold medal decoration continued in use until the 1930s. Horse and carts were also used for the bakery business which was very successful at that time.

Thomas & Evans show horse ready for the May Day Parade pictured outside the Pop Works in Jenkin Street, Porth, in the 1920s.

Three generations of Thomas & Evans transport against the evocative background of the Lewis Merthyr Colliery, 1980.

Gwilym William's Corona Pop Artist

Spending a couple of hours in the company of Gwilym Williams is quite an experience if you've never done it before. It's rather like attending a concentrated crash course on fifty years of company history, conducted by a gifted tutor who can reflect on his career with crystal clarity and relate it with warmth and humour. It is very possible that Gwilym Williams, now aged sixty-four, will be the last Corona employee to complete fifty years service with the company. He reached that milestone in September, and has entered his fifty first year in the same familiar surrounding of Porth, where he first started working for Thomas and Evans on 21 September 1930.

Nowadays, with the minimum school leaving age at sixteen, it is of course impossible for anyone to embark on a career with a chance of equalling this feat. It is most fitting that the Rhondda Valley should provide the backdrop for the final chapter of Gwilym's career with the company. For it was here that he was born and educated, and where he used to earn a few pence at weekend, by assisting in the Box Department at Porth, on the site of the present Porth Sales Unit.

When the opportunity came to join the company as a full time employee in the Box Department, with a promise of a move to the paint shop within a few months, Gwilym jumped at it. In fact he was so keen that he quit school a week early to make sure that nobody beat him to the job!

So for the princely sum of five bob a week, young Mr Williams joined the select band of worker engaged in making wooden crates by hand ... and they used to turn out around 250 a day! Then at last came the day when he was invited to join the staff in the paint shop – a job which he has cherished almost without a break, through five decades.

'But his early tasks lacked the creative flair for which he is so well known today. In fact, he was simply engaged in painting black chassis for both motorised vehicles and horse-drawn wagons.

He clearly recalls the vehicle strength of the company in the early 1930s.

There were 112 vehicles – mostly Guys, Morris and Daimlers,' he said. 'And we had between 150 and 160 horse-drawn wagons which we continued to use until the outbreak of war'. Working in close proximity to William Evans' imposing house in Porth meant that young Master Williams was frequently dispatched to the founder's home to turn his hand to a variety of odd jobs. He recalls one of the awesome aspects of these visits was the constant presence of William Evans' wife, Annie. 'She would take a chair and sit next to me and just talk, talk, talk,' he said. 'But being the boss's wife I was a bit scared to say anything, so we didn't have many memorable conversations'.

The expansion of the company in the 1930s meant a vast increase in the transport fleet, and Gwilym clearly remembers a newspaper picture of William Evans signing an order for 50 new Morris trucks. Expansion included buying existing businesses such as Edwards' bakery in Cardiff. And that meant repainting the entire Edwards fleet to match the Thomas and Evans livery. One of his few sorties away from the Valleys took him to Plymouth, where he remembers getting quite bored repainting the Devon and Cornwall fleet.

'I was quite an established sign-writer by this time, and I was getting a bit fed up just giving a facelift to old vehicles with a lick of paint,' he said. But he had little time to consider an alternative. The outbreak of war saw him called up into the Devon Regiment where, by his own admission, he had a pretty cushy time. 'I started off square bashing like everyone else, until they discovered I was a sign-writer. Then I had a marvellous time. They kept me painting all the time – anything from Divisional signs to "Keep off the Grass".' But Gwilym's skills failed to earn him even one stripe!

'They couldn't really promote me, because they were trying to hide me all the time. If I'd been promoted, they would have been over strength and I would have been transferred. It's a pity really – I often think I should have been a General'. Six years to the day after joining – 15 February 1946 – Gwilym was demobbed and dispatched back to Porth, where he opened up the Porth workshops, which had lain dormant during the war. Later that year he married his wife, Trephena, and the arrival of a son and daughter added a new dimension to their domestic life. For the past twenty-five years or more, Gwilym has dedicated himself to a variety of tasks, including rebuilding and painting an exact replica of one of Thomas and Evans' horse-drawn wagons, and, of course, completely refurbishing the pride of the Corona fleet – the 1927 Morris 'Z' Commercial vehicle. This recently won the highest possible accolade in the South Wales Historic Vehicles Show. And when away from his first love of restoring old vehicles – which isn't often – he devotes as much of his spare time as possible to the Rhondda Valley Amateur Boxing Club, of which he is chairman. Throughout the past half century, Gwilym Williams has painted himself into the pages of Corona's history. For he is as much a part of the Porth scene, as was William Evans when he was laying the foundations of today's Corona Empire. For as long as it is remembered that Corona started in Porth in the heart of the Rhondda, they will remember William Evans. And as long as old vehicles are around to provide a permanent reminder of those early days, people will remember the unassuming professionalizm and dedicated skills of the man who helped give them a new lease of life.

W. H. & E. G. Miles
7 New Houses, Dinas Road
Dinas, TONYPANDY
Mid Glam., CF40 1JG
Tel. 0443-663435

Issue No. 28
Autumn 1980

corona
news

THOMAS & EVANS L^{TD}

MORRIS

WK 3323

SALES AWARD

Luton do it again
Page Five

**GWILYM
WILLIAMS**
The pride of the
man who rebuilt
the pride of
the fleet —
Page Six

Gwilym Williams winning the cup for the Best Restored Wagon in the Corona fleet at the South Wales Historical Vehicle Show, 1980.

Some of Thomas & Evans' pop labels.

Millions of bottles and hundreds of thousands of cases are needed to satisfy the demand for 'Corona'. The upper photograph shows the Normal day-to-day requirements of an average factory. Bottles in their cases are awaiting passage through the washing plant, which is illustrated below.

Vehicles (above) and the serving unit (below) at the Welsh Hills Works, Jenkins Street, Porth. 'Corona' operated a large fleet of vehicles, familiar to many with their red and gold paint. Loading the lorries was performed by mechanical conveyors and the servicing of the entire fleet was carried out systematically in the firm's own engineering shop.

Comedian Dave King as featured in the early Corona Christmas television commercial.

GOLLY! IT AIN'T HALF WARM

What can you give the children, hot and tumbled with play, when they rush in for something to quench their burning thirst and cool their heated little bodies? Water isn't too safe and milk is unpalatable yet it's cruel to keep them long without something.

Give all active youngsters then, some of the many varieties of the famous

"Corona" Pure Drinks (in reputed quart bottles)

DELICIOUS, REFRESHING AND OF GREAT COOLING VALUE!

which will immediately quench their thirst, safely lower the temperature of the body and make them feel thoroughly pleased, satisfied and comfortable inside. Give them these drinks freely; they can do nothing but good. Non-alcoholic, they are absolutely pure, being made solely from choice fruit, refined sugar and carefully prepared aerated water

Guarantee : THE general excellence, purity and health-giving properties of these beverages are absolutely guaranteed by the Proprietors of the famous "WELSH HILLS" pure drinks (a brand you should ask for at Hotel, Restaurant or Refreshment House) who were, in LONDON AWARDED THE GOLD MEDAL, 1921 for the very high standard of manufacture of their products

THOMAS & EVANS, LIMITED
CARDIFF with branches all over Industrial Wales and head offices at PORTH

Corona children's advert showing the nutritious value and purity of the product.

Britain's Better Family Beverage

"CORONA"

HALF-PENNY STAMP

DELICIOUS DRINKS DELIVERED TO YOUR DOOR

Please call at—

Name ....

Address ....

......

Thomas & Evans, Ltd.,

"Corona" Stores,

London Road,

Dorchester

A sample of Corona's advertising literature

KINDLE YOUR ORDER EARLY.

"CORONA"
FOR CHRISTMAS

Bottles		
Sparkling Drinks Orange Crush, Lime Fruit & Soda, Crush, Dandelion & Burdock Lemon-Barley, Lemonade, etc.	Four Large Bottles **1/2**	
Delicious Cordials Lemon Squash, Lime, Black Currant Peppermint, Ginger 'B' etc., also Non-Alcoholic **Raisin & Ginger Wines**	Large Size Bottle **1/3**	
Pure Malt and Spiced Vinegar	large bottle **6½d**	

Plus 1d deposit on each bottle which is returnable.

'TERONA' TEA is an ideal Christmas Gift
a 1 lb. Canister costs 2/8

Trevor Howells on the left with foreman of the Paint Shop Gwilym Williams. Former employees of the Thomas & Evans Welsh Hills Works at the Monument to William Evans in Bronwydd Park.

Trevor Howells

Trevor Howells was born in Porth, Rhondda, in 1913. He left school at the age of fourteen years and he started work with Thomas & Evans Ltd in the Paint Shop as an apprentice painter. The workshop was opposite the Old Post Office in Porth. He was sent to London to do a further course in painting. In 1937 he was called up for the Army and he served with the 'Sherwood Foresters'. He fought abroad, he was captured by the Japanese in Singapore in 1941 and he was a prisoner of war for 3 1/2 years. After the war he came back to Porth to the firm of Thomas & Evans Ltd. where he remained for the rest of his working life. He served Thomas & Evans for fifty years and was presented with a gold wristwatch for his services, which were only broken by the time he spent in the Army.

A horse and cart entering Jenkin Street during the making of the television documentary programme by the BBC on Thomas & Evans, Prince of Porth.

A general view of the Welsh Hills Works being prepared for the television cameras.

Connie
Owens and
the BBC actor
portraying
William
Evans
pictured at
the Welsh
Hills Works,
Jenkin Street,
Porth.

A Corona
supervisor and
assistant
getting ready
to launch the
new baby pop!

A smart new image for the door-to-door salesmen and their delivery vehicles, 1950.

This impressive vehicle was designed exclusively for canvassing new door-to-door customers in the late 1950s.

'Building Beautiful Bodies'. Left to right: S. Williams, V. Rowlands (Foreman), F. Thomas, L. Kirk, K. Sheppard.

Harry Miles on his round in 1940. Harry started with Corona on the 14 April 1933 and worked until 31 April 1973.

Corona Workshop Boys, 1980. Left to right, back row: Elwyn Owens, Ian Jones, Ivor Wasley. Front row: Ken Gould, Cyril Savage, Stewart Barrett.

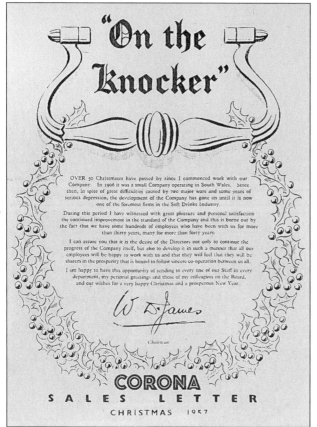

"On the Knocker"

OVER 50 Christmases have passed by since I commenced work with our Company. In 1906 it was a small Company operating in South Wales. Since then, in spite of great difficulties caused by two major wars and some years of serious depression, the development of the Company has gone on until it is now one of the foremost firms in the Soft Drinks Industry.

During this period I have witnessed with great pleasure and personal satisfaction the continued improvement in the standard of the Company and this is borne out by the fact that we have some hundreds of employees who have been with us for more than thirty years, many for more than forty years.

I can assure you that it is the desire of the Directors not only to continue the progress of the Company itself, but also to develop it in such a manner that all our employees will be happy to work with us and that they will feel that they will be sharers in the prosperity that is bound to follow sincere co-operation between us all.

I am happy to have this opportunity of sending to every one of our Staff in every department, my personal greetings and those of my colleagues on the Board, and our wishes for a very happy Christmas and a prosperous New Year.

W. D. James
Chairman

CORONA
SALES LETTER
CHRISTMAS 1957

Leaflets were put on the knocker of every door in the locality or advertize and promote Corona's Christmas delivery service.

Four

Sport and Leisure

Wilf and Menna Jones of Britannia, Porth.

More Memories by Wilf Jones
My Sporting Life 1920s and '30s

There was quite a variety of sport in the Rhondda Fach during this era. Porth had a good class football club. They played on Cae Mawr which also had a Greyhound racing rack. Strange as it may seem, there was no rugby club, but one of the finest players to grace a rugby field came from Porth, the legendary Cliff Jones, a Cambridge Blue and Welsh International. He later became President of the Welsh Rugby Union. There was a Cricket Club that had a good membership, also Bronwydd Bowls Club, their headquarters Bronwydd Park. The Hamer family that made a mark in the snooker world were well known throughout the Valley. Also the Datridge brothers in the same sport.

The village of Ynyshir was the home of six football teams. The Albions, Shamrocks, Spartans, Tigers, Linnets and Shoppies. The Shoppies played on Thursdays that was the early closing day in the Rhondda. One of the first professional footballers in the Rhondda was from Ynyshir by the name of Albie Mays. He signed for Bristol Rovers then transferred to Wrexham when he was capped for Wales. There was also a cricket team, also a runner by the name of Will George Matthews Welsh Cross Country Champion six times. All these sports had good support from the locals.

Wattstown also had its sporting fraternity. There was a good class football team, cricket team and a bowls club. Then in 1932 Wattstown Boys Club opened. They had three football teams, two senior sides and a junior side, gymnastics team, cross country team, basketball and indoor games team. In all sections they won trophies in the South Wales Federation of Boys Clubs Competitions. None more outstanding than the basketball team of 1936, which won the first Welsh Basketball Championship then went to London to play Hoylake, English Champions, but lost to them. Hoylake represented Great Britain in the 1936 Olympic Games in Berlin. There was also a quoits team in the village. There was an annual carnival, all sorts of entertainment. The main event was the road race. It was often won by Dickie Martin. Unfortunately he lost a leg in a colliery accident. When they had the next carnival he asked, 'How much start can I have?'

The village of Pontygwaith had a football team, The Stars. Also Penrhys Harriers Headquarters 'Penrhys Hotel' – long since demolished – two boxers Billy Fry and Evan Williams better known as 'Ianto Skint'.

Stanleytown, a village of five streets, also had a football team. Tylorstown was the home of a rugby club (formed in 1903), a soccer team and a family of boxers, Teddy, Ivor, Emlyn and Dickie Lewis. Dickie also played football for Tylorstown Albions. Jimmie Wilde was the Tylorstown Terror. Ferndale also had a rugby club, football club and some boxers. Blaenllechau, another small village, hosted a football team as did the last village, Maerdy.

The highlight of the football seasons was the cup competitions: the Hospital Cup and the Doctor Orr Cup. Of all the clubs in the Valley only two had proper dressing rooms, Porth and Wattstown. All the others used pubs as dressing rooms. It was a familiar sight to see 'Black Players' on the field of play. They weren't from foreign climates but men who worked in the pits and had no time to bath before playing. There was no financial benefits for players, they often paid their own tram fares to visiting games, often walking home enjoying a 'Trophy Doubler'. What is that you may ask? It was fish and chips. A large piece of fish 2d and a portion of chips 1d. You say they were lucky in those days, maybe so, but it was difficult to find 3d. Sport was played with satisfaction not for money.

Miners on strike formed "Catty and Dog" teams playing different streets. It was enjoyable while the strike lasted. Miners and their families were often short of money so times were very hard then.

Porth YMCA sports day and garden party, 1911.

Two early photographs of athletics and tug-of-war on Tynycymmer Estate, Porth, 1910.

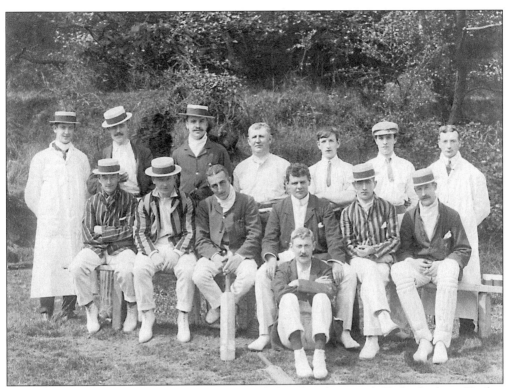

Porth Carnival cricket team in the 1920s. Included in the photograph Tudor Jenkins, Timber Yard Builders, Porth and Wayne Morgan who had a Club named after him in Trehafod.

The Wattstown Quoits team who were runners up 1929. In 1930 the team became champions. Note: does anyone know the whereabouts of the Quoits and the Trophies?

Ynyshir Albions pictured outside the Station Hotel, 1906/07.

Rhondda Transport AFC, 1936/37.

Ynyshir Albions League Champions, 1908/09.

Left: Tom Pike, a fine athlete and member of the basketball team which won the championship of 1936. *Right:* In memory of Rhondda's unknown sporting heroes. Young Schoolboy's First Welsh Cap, 1938.

Wattstown Rovers AFC pictured outside 'Grove House' overlooking the park, 1909/10.

Dinas Stars AFC outside the Dinas Arms Hotel, 1917. This shows how they kitted out the team and mascots.

Cymmer School football team, 1924/25.

Upton Rovers football team, Mount Pleasant, Porth, in the 1920s.

The Black Diamond AFC, 1933/34. The team is pictured wearing the kit of the Black Diamond Hotel, Trebanog.

Ynyshir Tigers AFC pictured at the back of the long gone Eagle Hotel, Ynyshir, 1937/38.

Porth County Boys rugby team, 1941/42.

Porth Secondary Girls hockey team, 1944/45. The headteacher was Tom Davies and the teachers were Miss Randall, Miss Rees Teachers seen here with Mary Evans (third from the left, back row).

Dinas Corries AFC, League Champions and Cup Winners, 1946/47.

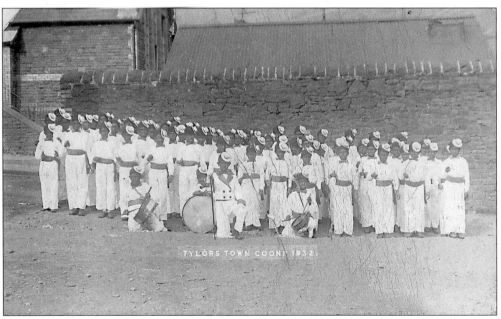

Tylorstown Coons Jazz Band preparing to go on parade at half time, 1932.

Viv Rowlands of Cymmer, Porth playing for Cardiff Schoolboys football in 1940.

Viv Rowlands as a professional footballer playing for Chelsea FC in 1949.

Viv Rowlands pictured on the third row, fifth from left with Chelsea Football Club, a First Division team, 1949/50.

Porth Weightlifting Team at Cymmer, 1955. David Hanks is in the back row, third from left and seventh from the left is Bruno Bertorelli. The man wearing a suit is Mr Davies, Manager of Lloyds Bank, Porth.

Glamorgan Champions, Ferndale School football team, 1954/55.

Lewis Merthyr billiards and snooker team, winners Pontypridd and District League, 1956.

Station Hotel, Ynyshir, darts team, 1958.

Rhondda County School Football Team, 1914/15.

Rhondda Transport cricket tam, 1960. Front row, second left is Vernon Fletcher, sixth left is Glyn Jones (captain) and next to him is Alfi Broad.

The ladies football team, Pembroke Street, 1953. Left to right, back row: Mrs Pring, Mrs Blackburn, Mrs Hicks, Mrs Brown, Mrs Buckley, Mrs Davies, Mrs Pring, Mrs Slade. Front row: Mrs Chapple, Mrs Griffiths, Mrs Christopher.

Wattstown Fun Run in the late 1950s. Pictured at Bailey Street outside the entrance to Wattstown Memorial Park.

Five

Dinas to Gilfach Goch

Hinds Pit, Dinas, which was sunk in 1851. The Tynewydd disaster was caused by water flooded through from this colliery in 1877.

Left: Jim Nagle of Cymmer Road dressed in authentic cowboy outfit, 1932. The horse, Shamrock, was stabled at Shoni Jones's farm, Graig Ddu, Dinas. *Right:* Laura 'Lolly' Evans (née Newmand). On the left hand side of photograph is Graig Ddu School and in the centre is Wain Arw Chapel.

The top end of Dinas with the turning on the right to Trealaw and the post office, 1900.

Mission Church Dinas which was built with corrugated iron. The church is still standing today.

Dinas Sunday School outside The Mission Church, 1960.

Left: William John Dent, a Charlie Chaplin impersonator, lived at Concrete Houses, Dinas. He was a member of the Humming Birds concert party at Central Hall, Porth. *Right:* 'A chapel invitation' to supper, 1910.

The shelter at Bronwydd Park, Porth, photographed in the late 1920s. This was donated to the people of Porth by William Evans.

'A Hot Summer's Day' in the 1930s at Porth Park Water Fountain. Catherine Nagle and Nelly Keohane are seen enjoying a refreshing drink.

The level being opened at Penygraig by striking miners during the Great Coal Strike of 1921.

Graig-yr-Eos Schools and general view of Penygraig, 1930s.

Penygraig Co-operative Carnival horse and cart, 1926.

Nantgwyn Colliery, Williamstown, sometime before 1900.

Williamstown School Standard 3A, 1927. Mr Kitchener Davies (seen on the right) was the first Welsh Nationalist Councillor in the Rhondda.

Williamstown School, 1934.

'The Church Lads Brigade', St Illtyd's Church, Williamstown, 1935.

James Prothero, Under Manager at Cilely Colliery, 1910.

Cilely Colliery, Tonyrefail, 1910.

Cwmlai School, Tonyrefail, 1931.

Pembroke Street, Tonyrefail, 1947.

Mill Street, Tonyrefail, in the 1940s. Forlini's Café on the corner.

Men and boys from Meyler and Pembroke Street bathing in the River Ely with the Old Imperial Hotel, Tonyrefail, top right.

Coronation Day, Pembroke Street, 1953. Included in the photograph are: Ray Ward, Freddie White, Brian Davies, Billy and Kenny Pring, Keith Hendy, Kenneth Jenkins, Billy Church, Mrs Taylor and Marion Taylor.

Trip to Barton Fair, September 1954. Left to right: Freddie White, Brian (Gomer) Davies, Ronnie Rees, Lawrence Brain.

A view overlooking Tonyrefail showing Tylcha Wen, Meyler Street, Tyn-y-Bryn, Collena Farms – now a housing estate – and Trebanog. Also the Old Railway Line from Pontyclun to Penygraig can be clearly seen. Left to right: Ronnie Rees, Brian Davies, Lawrence Brain.

Richard Williams MBE, LRAM (seen centre with his back to the camera) was the founder and music director of the Richard Williams Singers. Richard Williams was awarded the MBE in 1977 for his services to music. Prior to 1951 he was Principal Bass with the Welsh National Opera Company. After obtaining his licentiates of the Royal Academy of Music and Welsh College of Music and Drama, he entered the teaching profession in 1975.

The Richard Williams Singers have an international reputation that has taken them far and wide with appearances in Europe, the Soviet Union, the United States, Canada, France, Germany, Austria and Switzerland. They were privileged to perform in the presence of Queen Elizabeth, the Queen Mother at the official opening of St David's Concert Hall, Cardiff. Other members of the Royal Family to whom they have sung include Princess Diana and the Duke and Duchess of Kent.

Richard Williams Singers.

When Lunch time comes, a little Pastry
A tartlet sweet or something tasty.

HOW WE PASS THE TIME

AT TONYREFAIl.

A small collection of Victorian lithographic cards with a romantic theme for Valentine's Day.

HOW WE PASS
THE TIME
DOWN HERE

t this spot that no time we may miss,
We mostly start the day like this.

At night time when the shadows fall
Then, that's the sweetest time of all.

High Street, Gilfach Goch, in the 1940s. Lorenzo Bacchetta's Café was then opposite The Glamorgan Hotel.

Lorenzo Bacchetta and his ice cream cart, High Street, Gilfach Goch, 1920. He and brothers Giuseppi and Serafino (Sid) had shops in High Street, Evanstown and Garden City.

Left: Giuseppi Bacchetta, 1940. *Right:* Giuseppi Bacchetta back on the farm in Italy (Bardi).

The Little Italian Shop

In the little Italian shop
Where they sell coloured gassy pop,
Listen to Emlyn tell his mate
How to organize the State,
How to end the troublous days
And lead the world to wiser ways.
Danny bach Dwl is eager, too
To put an end to ballyhoo;
And Nipper Evans would put things right
In this nation overnight.
Over a steam pie and a glass of pop
One would make things brisk and hot,
Another kill the whole damn lot...
And on and on the chatter flows
Until Maria yawns and goes,
To pull the blinds and shut the shop
So full of coloured gassy pop.

Idris Davies

Vincenzo and Dominica Rinieri at the shop in High Street. Dominica is the daughter of Lorenzo Bacchetta.

115

Hendre Fadog School on the brow of the hill before you enter Garden City, Gilfach Goch, 1950. The teacher on the right hand side was married to Mr Bill Thomas the food inspector from Charles Street, Porth.

Dinas Main Colliery, Gilfach Goch, in the 1900s.

Britannic Colliery, Gilfach Goch, 1900. This colliery was made famous, not only for its coal output, but was used as a backdrop for the film *Proud Valley* starring Paul Robeson.

Trane and Llewellyn Pits, Gilfach Goch, 1934.

Left: Alice Hicks (née Barrow) in straw boater with sister Elsie Barrow and Kerry Dempsy. *Right:* Harry 'Dad' Hicks, Hillside Terrace, Wattstown, the brother of Aunt Alice, 1936.

Aunt Ali's Story

In the year 1903 I paid my first visit to Wattstown, Rhondda. My first impression was such, I never though I could come here to live. After a few months, I returned to Wales and took a place at Penarth as General Maid and lived there for over two years. Then I left to be married to Sidney John Hicks who lived in Wattstown he being a native of Dorset. He was a Widower with two children, a son, thirteen, and a daughter, ten.

Then, when we were able, we went to English Baptist. Then, after a time, we went to the Salvation Army at Porth. I became treasurer of the Women's Home League and we had Cottage meetings in our home. Mrs Mead, my next-door neighbour, got converted in one of these meetings. Then I started a Children's Service at our home and we had some very wonderful meetings. Then, on hearing there was a Children's Anniversary at the Institute Wattstown, I went on the Sunday morning and the chairman at that service was a young man who was leaving for Australia and he had worked hard for this Bethel Mission. His name was Johnnie Morris who lived over Ystrad. I heard many years after that this same Johnnie Morris was the president of the Baptist Union in that part of Australia. On that Sunday morning, at the service which was a farewell meeting day for him, he pleaded for workers for Bethel Sunday School and I responded to his call and that was how I came to go to Bethel, where we remained for many years and we got more to come and take an interest in the Church and School.

We started a building fund and had a women's sewing class. We met there each week. The first thing we made was a big rag mat which was sold for £1 1s. Then we each one made sets of curtain tie-ups and hair-tidies which we sold for 3s 6d, a set which helped the building fund to grow. Then the young people became very interested and they had their weekly meetings and then we started cantata and concerts. Mr Tom Evans, Bailey Street, was the conductor and organist. Then, one day, the news came to Thomas Bowen that there was a band room for sale at Abergary Colliery (1915). So three of us, Mr Bowen, Mrs T. Evans and I went over and saw the band room. We purchased it there and then through the Revd Harris. Then the work was begun and a place was found for us at the end of School Street. The councillors of that time did all they could. Also the owners of the National, the Watts Brothers, Mr John Kane, who was the Manager, allowed the band room to be brought over by rail to Wattstown National and Mr Griffin with helpers hauled it up in parts to the place where with additions, it still stands. We paid the big price of £5 for the band room. We were fifteen members when we started this building and we all worked and gave in every way possible. We employed a man to do carpentry then found out he wasn't very interested in doing his job, so he got a minute's notice. Then, another man came and our young men and women volunteered. When the roof was put on, each volunteer got a tin of paint and a brush which each paid for themselves. Women mostly painted the walls around while men painted the inside top and roof white.

Mr John Kane granted us paint for the outside of the building at cost price and we had many sheets of zinc and some timber. We had water laid on the outside, also had to have some lavatories built. Believe me, the men – Sidney Hicks, Octavious Jenkins and Ted Crew with others – dug down outside the building and dug up the stones to build the surrounding wall. A mason from Pontygwaith built the wall and Sidney Hicks acted as a labourer until the wall was finished. I should have said Jim Phillips of Hillside Terrace, also James Phelps Senior built the foundations for the building. Then when the church was ready to be opened, the cost was met from our own building fund with donations given. The cost was £58 and we had the Revd Mr Harris to consecrate and open Bethel Mission. It could never have been done as well, had it not been for prayer and unity, both with old and young people, members and non-members. For quite a long period, the women took it in turns to clean the Mission Church free. Then the time came when we were in a position to pay. Then Gran, Mrs Bowen, became caretaker and was paid one pound per month.

We had suffered the First World War and quite a few of our lads went and we kept in touch with them by writing and sending parcels to them. We were glad to welcome them back after the war. Then came the 1926 strike lasting for six months. Every morning during the strike we held a Prayer Meeting at six o'clock. Much blessing was received at those meetings to all who attended them. Sometime later, we had a fortnight's mission by Miss Philpott of Lanllety and Mr Brinley Evans of Ferndale. Quite a few were converted and became members. One outstanding character was Mr Watkin Mainwaring who did much work in the Church. He became conductor and organist and treasurer of the church until he passed away in 1960. Much tract distributions were made to every house in Wattstown. The men and women held open-air meetings every week. The teacher was Superintendent, Mr T. Bowen. We carried banners, left cards and sang, visiting every street then back to the Mission for tea. Then afterwards, up the mountain for games and races for the children.

Our Mission had become too small though, and the church meeting in 1925 passed a proposal to make an extension. We did, the cost being over £100. It was paid for and we had a new organ costing £27. This was lent to the church by a member, free of interest until such time it could be paid back which was within a year. At that time there was much poverty in South Wales and many very poor people in Wattstown. We felt we must follow Dorcas's example and started a sewing class. Two of us went to the Pontypridd market and bought some material to make up some clothes for children. We made up three lots of maternity bags and two women were picked to take charge of these bags. They consisted of garments for the mother use, also for baby. They were allowed to use them for two or three months. When they were returned to the sister in charge they were made ready for the next. We really felt we were doing the practical Christian work. But some men and a couple of women decided it was to stop and we felt it must be carried on. It resulted in me coming out of Bethel but I still carried on the sewing class in the Institute and the women came there to sew and we carried on till times were brighter. I and my husband went to Carmel Church for a while, just a couple of Sundays but we had no intention of being members there. But we really were caught as the Welsh Chapel was in much debt at that time.

The Heads of Welsh Independent Church decided they were willing to turn it into English until such time as they were free from debt, which never came. One Sunday evening, we went there and the deacons asked us both to come and help them to build the church up with them and the members of Carmel. We felt it impossible to refuse and we did our little, as best we could. They flourished for a few years and we had some very good times. We started a sisterhood and had a growing Sunday School. Then I returned back to Bethel and after three months I was made a member again. I was asked to take back the sisterhood and my class of girls and we worked together for a few years. Many of the older members had passed away.

One of the men who came from Ystrad was a Mr Minty and he travelled over for many years. Also a few young men started their preaching at Bethel: Revd M. Jones, Mr Ted Bevan, Mr Marchmond, Mr J. Drummond, Mr Roderick and W.J. Phillips and Mr Richard Davies. They all gave much service to the Lord in Bethel. There are quite a few I have forgotten so they must forgive me but everyone was very interested in each department. Some are still in the good work: Mr Frank Vaughan, Mr Starr, Mr Hugh Barrow, Mr Tom Evans, Mr J. Clement, Mr Evan Thomas, Mr David Rowlands, Mr Sidney Hicks, Mr Oliver Draisey, Mr Thomas Bowen, Mr Johns, Mr John Norris, Mr George Manders, Mr R. Davies, Mr Mainwaring, Mr Ernest Hicks. Mr Lewis Smith held position of Pastor for a few years.

Much good has been done and still is from the Bethel on the hill. In 1933 the roof was removed and a plain one, covering the whole of Bethel was put on. The freehold was purchased in 1945. Mr Manders was a god carpenter. He made a pulpit then a few years later he improved on it and made a bigger pulpit which still stands. Also he built cupboards which the sisterhood paid for. They also gave two armchairs for the pulpit and a clock which was used many years. Many children were christened in Bethel. The first person was Mrs Manders. She was a good worker when health allowed. She suffered and was unable to attend communion and Mr John would visit and give it to her when she was ill. I used to visit with him, those who were members. We had meetings at Gran Morgans, 29 Hillside Terrace. Her favourite Hymn was *Joyful will the meeting be*. She was a dear Christian. Also, she had asked for me to pray with her and the Matron would not allow it, she said if she needed anyone the Vicar could come. The old lady was very disappointed. Thank God, things are different today.

Arthur Phillips, Chapel Street, was one of our scholars and he was only twelve years of age. They sent for me one morning. He was dying and I shall never forget him. He was praying 'Oh God thou Son of David, have mercy on me and let me live for my mother'. 'I want to help my mother'. I asked him to say, 'Thy will be done' and he said, 'Thy will be done – but I would like to live for my mother'. His mother was a widow.

We had quite a few young scholars pass away and we always sent a wreath from the Sunday School. One thing, Mr Thomas Bowen was always good with the children. I never knew anyone who trusted the scholars good, as he did. Some are walking around today who will bare me out.

Mrs Rathbourne from Ferndale came for a period and took over the singing for the anniversaries. She was very good, also Eva and Reggie. They'd travel one night in the week to have practice, also on Sunday afternoons. Then, the Anniversary Services were held at the Institution and the hall would be packed. Everyone enjoyed listening to the children. Mr Rathbourne was one of our Preachers coming about every fourth or fifth Sunday.

Alice Mary Crawford Hicks (née Barrow), was born on 21 July 1887, at Evercreech, Somerset. She married Sidney John Hicks on 12 April 1909 when he was thirty-seven years old and she was twenty-one years old. The marriage was solemnised at the parish church of Penarth Glamorgan, South Wales. Witnesses were Evelyn May Crawford Barrow (sister and my mother) and Mr Hugh Crawford Barrow (brother and father of Cynthia, Hugh and Billy my cousins). The curate who performed the ceremony was Mr Howard C. Morliuw.

Aunt Ali suffered greatly especially during her last years. Cancer, the removal of a breast she was never free from pain. Diabetes set in and she gradually became more frail and weak. But she never lost her courageous spirit or her everlasting faith in God. She was honest, hardworking, a Christian woman, most of all, one of those unique beings within a family, a dear, kind and much loved aunt.

God's Word gave her hope and strength.
Her life was sharing and helping in the love of God.

In the beginning was the Word … At her ending … God's Word was 'Peace'.

Six
Ynyshir
and Wattstown

Ynyshir Road looking south, 1920.

Ynyshir Infants School, 1936.

Moriah chapel Sunday School, Ynyshir, on a trip to Barry Island, seen here outside Barry railway station, 1938.

Mr and Mrs Mary Ann and David Davies pictured in the garden at the rear of their house-cum-shop at 66 Taff Street, Ferndale, in 1920. Mrs Davies' father and mother were the cook and gardener at Ferndale House.

'Our Gang' looking down from Llanwonno Road on the Oval, Ynyshir, 1940/41. Included in the photograph are: Miss Jackson, Cul Hanks, H. Evans, G. Stevens, I. Wathan, D. Jackson, D. Roberts, H. Wathan. Three of the children in the front row (first, second and fifth from the left) were evacuees. The dog belonged to a local coal merchant.

Elder members and trustees of Ynyshir St Johns Ambulance Brigade pictured in the Ambulance Hut, Llanwonno Road, 1953.

William Morgan aged sixty, David Hanks aged two, Myrddin Hanks aged six at back of 5 Weston Terrace, Ynyshir, 1930. William Morgan died in 1947, David Hanks died in 1990, Myrddin Hanks retired as a Major from the RWF.

Left: The Kingsbury family, Heath Terrace, Ynyshir. The young boy on the right is Percy Kingsbury, a fine Rhondda athlete and rugby player. *Right:* Gil Hanks, Gun Sergeant 37th HAA stationed at Germany.

Left: Mr Jack Jones, Edmund Street, Wattstown, 1927. He worked in Tylorstown colliery and was killed in France on 25 July 1917. *Right:* Mrs Williams of Aberllechau Road, Wattstown, in the 1920s.

Mr Daniel Philips and his milk cart on Victoria Terrace, Wattstown, in the 1920s.

Wattstown Colliery, August 1953. Left to right, back row: Reg Brown, Will Phillips, Alun Evans, Edgar Richardson, Will Stuckey, Tom Stevens. Front row, sitting: Randy Stroud, Tommy Griffiths, Len Davies, Jim Darby.

A scholarship class from Aberllechau Road, Wattstown, in 1936. The headmaster, Mr Morgan is on the left and the teacher, Miss Rowlands is on the right.

Three Rhondda boys looking for talent at the Rink Ballroom, Porth. They are Malcolm Griffiths, Bill Cooksley and Tom Evans.

George Hicks is seen here with a bike; the Scout is Will Hicks, the boy is Joe Hicks and the little girl is Marie Hicks. They are pictured with their dog Bob outside Woodland Cottage, Hillside Terrace, Wattstown, 1920.

Acknowledgements

Margaret Millington, Nell Davies, Connie Owens, Bill Murphy, Gerald Hughes, Alan Phillips, Rhys Owens, Group Captain D.T. Owens, John Nagle, Steve Ferrari, Pino Rinieri, Giulia Young, Brian Davies, Anthea Davies, Lui Bacchetta, Brenda Saunders, Gwyn Harries, Sylvia Briar, Roy Hicks, Beryl Trinder, Jean Curtis, John and Paul Poole, Morg. Davies, Florence Fletcher, Sarah Morgan for her Secretarial and Computer Work, John Thomas, Alan Williams, Pastor Ed. Moore, Rev. Keith Phillips, Margaret Rudd, Terry Edwards.

Special Thanks To: Wilf Jones, Andrew Penhaligan, Harry Miles, Mr and Mrs Edwin (Australia), Allan Rogers M.P., Selwyn Davies.